AN UNOFFICIAL GUIDE FOR FORTNITE FANS

HACKS FOR FORTNITERS

SURVIVING AND WINNING 50 V 50 MATCHES

AN UNOFFICIAL GUIDE FOR FORTNITE FANS

HACKS FOR FORTNITERS

SURVIVING AND WINNING 50 V 50 MATCHES

AN UNOFFICIAL GUIDE TO TIPS AND TRICKS THAT OTHER GUIDES WON'T TEACH YOU

JASON R. RICH

Sky Pony Press
New York

Visit our website at www.skyponypress.com.

10 9 8 7 6 5 4 3

Library of Congress Cataloging-in-Publication Data is available on file.

Series design by Brian Peterson

Print ISBN: 978-1-5107-4456-1
Ebook ISBN: 978-1-5107-4464-6

Printed in China

TABLE OF CONTENTS

AN UNOFFICIAL GUIDE FOR FORTNITE FANS

HACKS FOR FORTNITERS

SURVIVING AND WINNING 50 V 50 MATCHES

SECTION 1
PREPARE FOR THE ULTIMATE 50 V 50 BATTLE EXPERIENCE

Have you already experienced the excitement of playing *Fortnite: Battle Royale*'s Solo, Duos, and/or Squads game play modes? If so, you know that to achieve #1 Victory Royale, it's necessary to juggle more than a dozen different responsibilities in order to stay alive and defeat your enemies.

When playing a Solo match, it's your soldier against up to 99 others in a battle for survival. Duo mode allows you to team up with one other gamer and take on up to 98 other enemies in your quest for #1 Victory Royale. In Squads mode, you're able to team up with three other gamers (either your online friends or random players) as you fight up to 96 enemies with the goal of outlasting everyone else during a match.

The Solo, Duos, and Squads game play modes are all permanently offered in *Fortnite: Battle Royale.* Choose which you want to experience from the Choose Game Mode screen.

Get Ready to Experience a 50 v 50 Match

In addition to the three permanent game play mode options, Epic Games often offers one or more temporary game play modes—including a version of 50 v 50. When you select this mode, during each match, there are two teams, each with 50 players. There are the blue and red teams, and you've been recruited into the blue team.

Playground mode is another temporary mode that comes and goes from the game. It gives you up to 55 minutes per session to explore, build, practice using weapons, and/or participate in mock battles with friends.

The goal of a 50 v 50 match is to help your team outlive the other, while contending with a storm that's more lethal than ever. Of course, the ultimate goal is to achieve #1 Victory Royale. Do you have the skill and determination to help lead your team to success?

When you experience a 50 v 50 match, there are more opportunities to find and collect weapons, ammo, loot items, and resources, compared to other game play modes. Supply Drops, for example, appear much more frequently, but only within the circle which appears on the Island Map once the soldiers have all departed their respective Battle Buses.

Powerful Weapons and Intense Battles Can Be Found within the Circle

As soon as everyone lands on the island, the island map automatically transforms. Instead of showing the travel route of the Battle Buses, it'll display the border that divides the island into each team's side, as well as a circle that will eventually become the epicenter of battle toward the end of the match. In the meantime, it's exclusively within the circle where Supply Drops will land.

To obtain the best weapons and loot items, you'll want to venture into the circle. However, this is the location where soldiers from both teams are most apt to cross the border and meet, so you can always expect a fight here. As the storm moves and expands, it'll eventually center around the circle, and then slowly encompass it during the End Game.

By approaching the border at any point on the island, you'll likely encounter at least a few enemies, so be prepared for that. However, it's within the circle where soldiers (from both teams) who are looking for combat action will congregate.

50 v 50 Matches Are Unlike All Other Matches

During a 50 v 50 match, you'll definitely need the extra firepower and building capabilities, because these matches are faster paced than any other. Each time Epic Games introduces a new 50 v 50 match, there's often some unique twist that keeps things new and challenging.

Unlike other game play modes, when a 50 v 50 match begins, it takes longer for the storm to form and expand. During the first 10 minutes or so of each match, the weather will be clear, and the entire island remains inhabitable. Once the storm begins to devastate the island, however, it moves quickly and causes more damage faster to anyone who gets caught within it. As you're freefalling toward the island, you'll see a message in the center of the screen announcing that the countdown to the storm's formation has begun.

After choosing the 50 v 50 game play mode, your soldier gets transported to the pre-deployment area. If you're playing a 50 v 50 Squads game, for example, it's here you can meet up with your three squad members for the first time within the game. Use this time to choose a landing spot on the island.

Your choice of landing spots should be based on your overall objective for early in the match. Land near the border (particularly within the circle) if you want to encounter enemies quickly and engage in combat. Land on your side of the island, but farther away from the border, if you want extra time to build your arsenal and collect resources without the threat of enemies. If you're really looking for a challenge, consider landing in the heart of enemy territory (across the border within the other team's side of the island).

By checking the island map while waiting in the pre-deployment area, you'll discover the island is randomly divided in half. Each team (comprised of 50 soldiers) will be transported to their half of the island on their own Battle Bus.

Upon leaping from the Battle Bus, your soldier will freefall downward. Choose a desired landing location and aim for it. While you can land anywhere on the island, it's much safer to land on your team's half of the island so you have time to gather weapons, ammo, loot items, and resources before confronting enemies. For each match, the island is randomly divided in half at a different angle, and the Battle Buses will fly over each team's half of the island. The border is displayed as a dashed white line on the island map.

Who's a friend and who's a foe? As you explore the island, soldiers with a white arrow icon above their head are allies (your team members). Everyone else is an enemy!

As always, when you reach the island, your soldier is armed only with their trusty pickaxe. Assuming you landed a decent distance away from the border that divides the island, your first objective is to begin building your personal arsenal. Start collecting weapons, ammo, loot items, and resources.

Opening chests is one way to gather the weapons and loot items you'll need.

To gather more powerful weapons, larger collections of ammo, and bigger bundles of resources, as well as rare loot items, locate and open Supply Drops. These only appear in the circle that's displayed on the map. As the match progresses, the circle becomes a meeting point for the two teams, and is where the intense battles and the most building take place, especially during the End Game portion of the match.

Even though about half of the island is populated by your fellow team-mates, everyone wants to gather the best collection of weapons, ammo, and loot items possible, so if you're not the first person to explore an area, chances are it'll be picked over, and the best stuff will already have been taken by others. If you don't need something you find when exploring your half of the island, leave it for a teammate to grab.

As the storm expands, it'll push all soldiers remaining alive—from both teams—toward a Final Circle. This is where the final battles will take place. Once you've built up your personal arsenal, to help your team out the most, start heading toward the Final Circle, and be prepared to engage in massive, multi-soldier firefights.

You don't need to wait for the storm to push you into the circle. You can enter it at any time if you're seeking the rewards offered by Supply Drops, and you're willing to confront the danger of enemy encounters.

As soldiers (allies and enemies) are eliminated from the match, everything the defeated soldier previously collected gets left behind. This provides a perfect opportunity for you to upgrade your personal arsenal and expand your ammo and loot item collection. You just need to get close to the "hot zone," where battles between both teams are already taking place.

You may have the urge to engage in firefights and prove your worth by defeating as many enemies as possible, but you're also rewarded for reviving injured teammates, even if the injured soldier is not a squad member (if you're playing a 50 v 50 Squads match).

Fortnite: Battle Royale Hacks—Surviving and Winning 50 v 50 Matches focuses on helping you prepare to experience these fun and fast-paced 50 v 50 matches. This unofficial guide offers hundreds of proven strategies that'll teach you how to help your team win!

Experiencing a 50 v 50 match allows you to find and collect legendary weapons and loot items (these have an orange hue) that are typically very rare and very hard to come across in other game play modes. Plus, you have about 10 minutes before the storm approaches to explore the island. Playing a 50 v 50 match also increases your chances of engaging in successful battles so you can boost your soldier's Experience Points faster, while having allies all around you who can revive your soldier if he/she gets injured.

Be Ready to Juggle Many Responsibilities, Not Just Fight!

You're about to experience one of the most popular games in the world, and one of the most successful in gaming history. *Fortnite: Battle Royale* is a combat-oriented action/adventure that takes place on a mysterious island.

To become a pro, you'll need to handle many responsibilities at once, related to exploration, fighting, building, and survival. In other words, be prepared to:

1. Safely explore your team's half of the island or risk your safety and infiltrate the enemy's side of the island.
2. Avoid the deadly storm. When playing a 50 v 50 match, spending time in the storm causes a lot more damage than usual, so this is not someplace you want to get caught.
3. Harvest and collect resources, including wood, stone, and metal.
4. Locate, collect, and manage your personal arsenal of weapons. Knowing that you'll soon be facing many enemies, think about if you want to engage in close-range combat, mid-range combat, or long-distance combat, and build up your arsenal accordingly.
5. Find and collect plenty of ammunition for the types of weapons you'll be using. There are five types of ammunition, each works with different types of weapons. A weapon that runs out of ammunition is worthless.
6. Acquire and properly use loot items that can help you survive.

7. Manage the inventory in your soldier's backpack (which only has six slots capable of holding weapons and/or loot items, including your soldier's pickaxe).

8. Build ramps, bridges, structures, and fortresses using collected resources in order to reach otherwise inaccessible locations, or to provide defensive shielding during attacks.

9. Engage in combat with enemy soldiers.

10. Gather what you'll need for the End Game, as you enter into the Final Circle.

11. Revive your team members who get injured, before their Health meter gets fully depleted and they're eliminated from the match. Remember, you're rewarded for helping others, just as you're rewarded for defeating enemies.

12. When necessary share weapons, ammo, loot items, and resources with your teammates, or at least avoid grabbing everything you can find while leaving others with little or nothing worthwhile.

Customize Your Soldier's Appearance

If you're a fashion-conscious gamer, then in addition to performing well in a game, you probably want your character to look amazing too. Every day, Epic Games offers a new collection of ways to customize the appearance of your soldier. This is done using optional outfits, back bling designs, pickaxe designs, glider designs, contrail designs, and emotes.

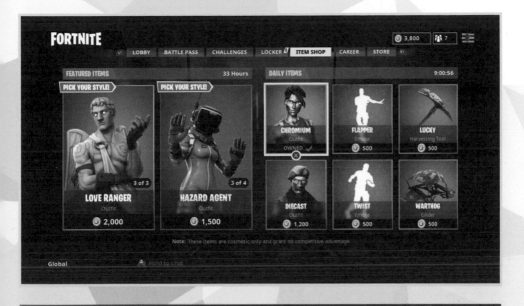

There are several ways to acquire these items. You can purchase them from the Item Shop, unlock them by completing Battle Pass challenges as you're playing *Fortnite: Battle Royale*, or obtain them as part of a Twitch Prime Pack (which requires you to be an Amazon Prime member and have a Twitch.tv account). From the Store section of the game, a Starter Pack that includes one exclusive outfit is often offered for $4.99 (US), which includes a bundle of 600 V-Bucks.

No matter how lit or powerful your soldier winds up looking after customizing his or her appearance, it's important to understand that all of these optional items are for cosmetic purposes only. None actually make your soldier faster, stronger, more powerful, or give them any competitive advantage within the game whatsoever. Despite this, gamers really enjoy customizing the appearance of their soldiers, and then showcasing their personality within the game using emotes.

Some outfits and related items are considered "legendary," meaning they're rare, limited-edition, and only available for a short time. Shown above are a few examples, including Magnus, Oblivion, Carbide, and Flytrap.

A few outfits, like Raven, will make your soldier look sinister, and will help to strike fear into your enemies, especially if you're a skilled *Fortnite: Battle Royale* player.

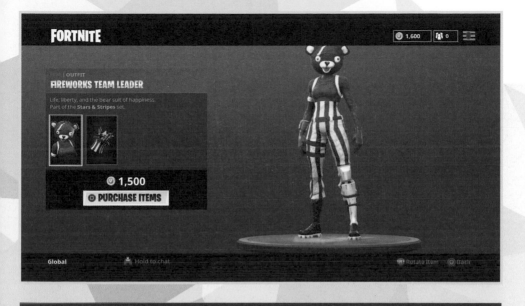

Other outfits and accessories are released in conjunction with an event happening in the game or a real-world event (such as this Fireworks Team Leader outfit, which was originally released around July 4th).

Toxic Trooper and Teknique were two theme-based outfits. Teknique, for example, was released at the same time Epic Games introduced spray paint tag emotes into the game.

And then there are whimsical outfits that are just fun to show off, like Cuddle Team Leader and Tomatohead.

For almost every outfit Epic Games releases, matching items, including a backpack design (back bling), pickaxe design, and glider design are also made available, but are typically sold separately.

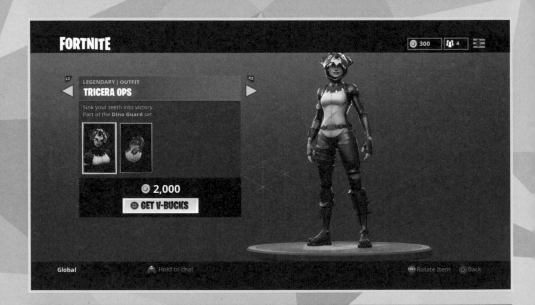

Some outfits, like Tricera Ops, get bundled with a matching backpack design at no additional cost, but these tend to be the outfits that cost 2,000 V-Bucks.

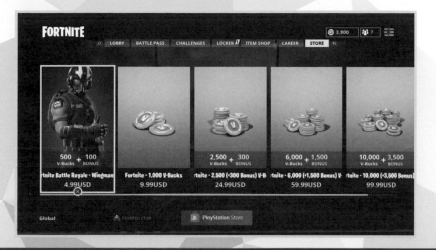

Outfits and related items acquired from the Item Shop cost money. You'll need to purchase V-Bucks (game currency) from the Store, and then use V-Bucks to purchase items one at a time from the Item Shop.

V-Bucks are also used to purchase a Battle Pass each season, or to unlock Battle Pass Tiers without having to complete the challenges associated with them in order to unlock the prize for that tier.

Plan on spending between $8.00 and $20.00 (US) per outfit, plus additional money for the related accessories. V-Bucks are sold in bundles. The larger bundle you buy, the bigger discount you get when you use them to purchase items. An outfit that costs 2,000 V-Bucks equates to about $20.00 (US).

Once you acquire items from the Item Shop or unlock them within the game, they are yours to keep forever, and each becomes available from the Locker. Prior to a match, access the Locker to mix and match the items you've purchased, acquired, or unlocked in order to give your character a truly unique appearance. From below the Emotes heading on the left side of the Locker screen, choose up to six different emotes. This is shown above.

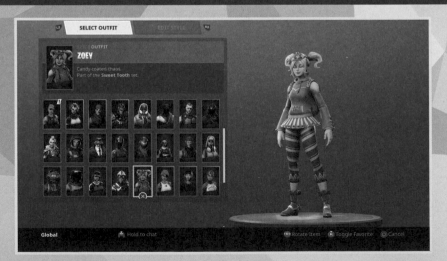

One at a time, from the Locker, select your soldier's outfit, back bling design, pickaxe design, glider design, and contrail design. Shown here, the Outfit slot of the Locker has been selected. This allows you to choose from the outfits you've previously purchased, acquired, or unlocked.

Emotes Allow You to Showcase Attitude and Personality

While in the pre-deployment area, or anytime during a match, you're able to publicly show off some attitude and personality by allowing your character to use one of three types of emotes.

When you choose a graphic icon emote, your soldier tosses an icon into the air for everyone around to see. The icon is displayed for a few seconds and then disappears. There are many different icons that can be unlocked, acquired, or purchased.

Using virtual spray paint, apply a spray paint tag to any flat surface within the game, such as on a wall of any structure.

There are many spray paint tags to choose from. Apply one at a time.

Mix and match a few spray paint designs to create some awesome-looking graffiti during your stay on the island.

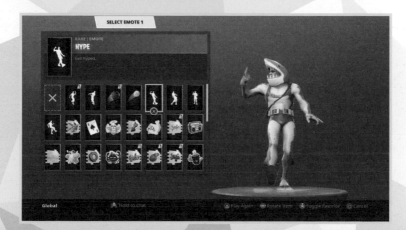

The third and most popular type of emote is a dance move. There are hundreds available, although you can only store six at a time. Showcase one dance move or use two or three back-to-back to demonstrate some lil choreography.

Once you've selected up to six emotes for your soldier, while in the pre-deployment area (shown here) or during a match, access the Emotes Menu to choose and showcase one of the up to six emotes you've preselected. All other nearby players will see it.

Some gamers use emotes during the game as a greeting when they encounter team members or allies. Others use them to taunt adversaries, or to gloat after badly injuring or defeating an enemy. Just remember, when you're using emotes, you can't also use a weapon or build, so your soldier is temporarily vulnerable.

Two of the emotes you can unlock are a golf ball and a basketball. If you have access to one or both of these emotes, from the Locker, add them to your emotes menu prior to a match.

During a match, if you want to waste some time, and you happen to be near the Lazy Links golf course or one of the more than ten basketball courts on the island, select one of these two emotes from the emotes menu.

You can now play a round of golf using your pickaxe as a golf club, or shoot some hoops on your own or with your teammates.

While playing golf or shooting hoops is a fun activity, it does leave your soldier vulnerable to attack and offers no tactical advantage whatsoever. You can also toss basketballs or shoot golf balls pretty much anywhere on the island you happen to be.

How to Adjust the Game's Settings and Options

When it comes to adjusting the in-game settings, there are a few that you definitely want to tweak in order to improve your game play experience.

Audio								

Volumes

Music Volume	0.23
SoundFX Volume	0.74
Voice Chat Volume	0.62
Cinematics Volume	0.50

Toggles

Subtitles	◄	On	►
Voice Chat	◄	On	►

Global   Hold to chat   Back

Since sound effects play such a critical role in the game, access the Audio submenu, and then turn down the Music Volume option. Turn up the Sound FX Volume option. If you're using a gaming headset to communicate with other players, also turn up the Voice Chat Volume and turn on and customize the various Voice Chat features. These options will vary, based on which gaming platform you're using. When playing a 50 v 50 match, it's most important that you're able to clearly hear all of the game's sound effects during matches.

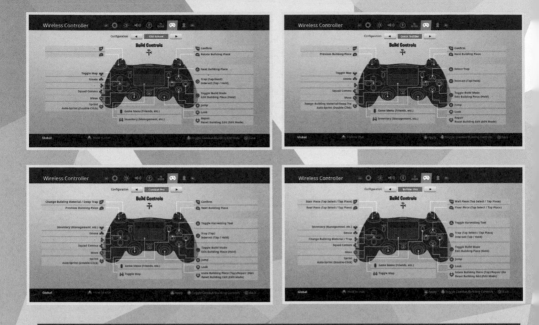

If you're playing *Fortnite: Battle Royale* on a console-based gaming system or have an optional controller connected to your computer, based on your personal gaming style and skill level, choose a Controller Layout that'll work best for you. Your options include: Old School, Quick Builder, Combat Pro, and Builder Pro. PC and Mac gamers can access the game's Input menu and assign each keyboard key and mouse button to perform specific game-related functions. These controller layouts are for a PS4. Similar options are available from the Xbox One and Nintendo Switch version of the game.

The default controller layout is called Old School. Stick with this one until you've gotten good at playing *Fortnite: Battle Royale* and you've developed your personal play style. If you tend to focus on building, for example, choose the Pro Builder layout. If your focus during matches is mainly fighting, choose the Combat Pro layout. Which one you select is purely a matter of personal preference.

When playing *Fortnite: Battle Royale* on a mobile device, access the HUD Layout tool to customize the on-screen controls for Combat and Build mode. You're able to customize the size and location of control-related icons that appear on the screen, based on how you hold your smartphone or tablet. Shown here on an iPad Pro.

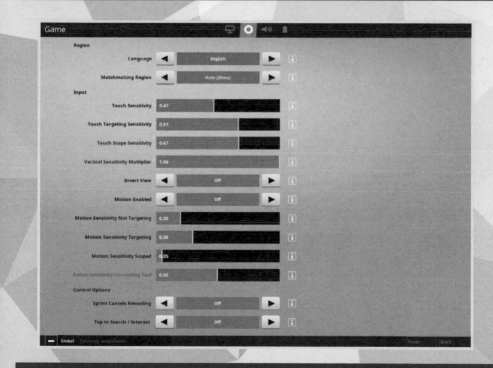

From your mobile device's main Game menu, select the Audio submenu to customize the game's audio options. Just as with all other versions of the game, there's also an extensive Game Settings menu, with individual options you can adjust. Shown here on an iPad Pro.

Customizing the look of your character, and then adjusting the game-related settings are all done by accessing options available from the Lobby. When these tasks are done, return to the Lobby, access the Choose Game Mode menu, select the 50 v 50 game play mode, and then from the Lobby, choose the Play option to enter into a match and proceed directly to the pre-deployment area. Remember, a continuous Internet connection is required to play *Fortnite: Battle Royale*.

SECTION 2
WELCOME TO THE MYSTERIOUS ISLAND

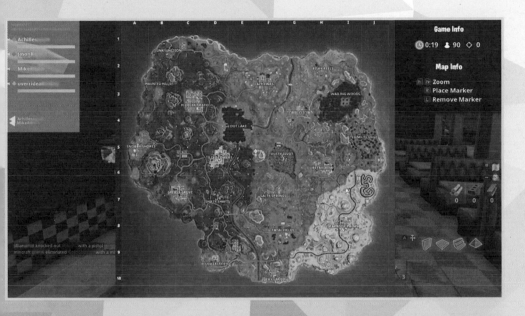

In addition to the approximately 20 labeled points of interest on the island map, you'll discover many additional (albeit smaller) locations that are not labeled. These too are well worth visiting, especially if they happen to be on your way to the circle when playing a 50 v 50 match. Almost every week or two, when Epic Games releases a game patch, something new is added to the island map, or existing locations are altered in some minor way. This is what the island map looked like part-way through Season 5. Each time a new season kicks off, expect some major geographic changes to occur on the island.

You Can Learn a Lot from the Island Maps

There are several versions of the island map you need to become acquainted with.

Continuously displayed on the screen during a match is the Location Map. It shows a small area of the island around your current location. Your exact location is displayed as a white triangle. All of your team-mates are displayed as blue triangles. If you're playing a 50 v 50 Squads game, your squad mates are displayed as different colored triangles. Depending on which gaming platform you're using, where this map is displayed on the screen will vary. It's shown here on a PS4, in the top-right corner of the screen. Remember, you can't ever see the location of your enemies on any map.

If you see a white line linked with your location icon (the white triangle) on the Location Map (shown) or island map, this is the path to follow to reach the circle, which transforms into an intense battleground part-way through each 50 v 50 match.

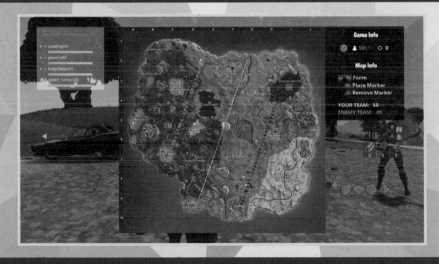

During the time you're in the pre-deployment area waiting to board the Battle Bus, or for the first 20 seconds or so that you're riding the bus, access the large island map to see how the island has been divided, and the random routes the two Battle Buses will be taking over the island. Knowing this can help you choose a landing location. (Remember, you're always placed on the blue team.)

Checking the island map during a match reveals a lot of useful information.

Here's what you can see on the island map during a match:

- The border between your team's side of the island and the enemy team's territory. This is the white line (made up of dashes) that cuts through the center of the island.

- The location of the circle, which is where many Supply Drops fall during a 50 v 50 match. This is also where many soldiers from both teams wind up confronting each other as the match progresses and the storm covers much of the island.

- The random routes the Battle Buses will take across the island. These routes are only displayed while you're in the pre-deployment area and for the first few seconds while aboard the Battle Bus.

- The location of each point of interest on the island.

- Your current location.

- The location of your team members (up to 49 of them), as well as the location of your Squad members (if you're playing a 50 v 50 Squads match).

- The current location of the storm. The storm-ravaged areas are displayed in pink.

- The progress and growth of the storm as it travels toward the circle and then shrinks around the circle.

- If markers have been placed on the map, these too are displayed. Colored flares will also appear on the main game screen. Use the marker/flare to set a meet-up location anytime during a match. Only you and your teammates can see a marker/flare.

After about 10 minutes, the storm begins to expand and move. Check the timer (displayed directly below the Location Map) frequently to determine when the storm will begin expanding, and make sure you avoid it.

Remember, the storm moves faster than your soldier can run, so unless you have an All Terrain Kart, Shopping Cart, Bouncer Pads, Launch Pads, and/or plan to find and use Rifts, or a Rift-to-Go, don't plan on trying to outrun the storm if you need to cover a long distance. Unlike when playing *Fortnite: Battle Royale*'s other game play modes, after the initial warning when your soldier lands on the island, no warnings are given when the storm expands and moves. You need to keep your eye on the Location Map and island map to see it.

Learn How Map Coordinates Work

Whenever you look at the large island map, you'll discover it's divided into quadrants. Along the top of the map are the letters "A" through "J." Along the left edge of the map are the numbers "1" through "10." Each point of interest or location on the map can be found by its unique coordinates.

For example, Tilted Towers is found at map coordinates D5.5, and Snobby Shores is located at coordinates A5. At the start of Season 5,

Paradise Palms replaced Moisty Mire and was centered around map coordinates I8, while Anarchy Acres was replaced by Lazy Links at map coordinates F2.5. The unlabeled Viking village (which contains the Viking ship) can be found on a mountaintop near map coordinates B4.5.

Hiding Behind Some Objects Offers Protection Against Incoming Attacks

Once you begin to explore the island, you'll discover it contains many different types of terrain. Wherever you happen to be, use your natural surroundings to your advantage. For example, climb up onto something to gain a height advantage or hide behind something for protection. Try to discover creative ways to use your natural surroundings.

If there's a mountain within or near the circle, or near the border on your team's half of the island, this is a good spot to build a fort so you have protection when you shoot downwards at your enemies who are below.

When you're traveling on foot, you always have the option to crouch down and use nearby objects as shielding from an incoming attack or to hide from enemies in hopes of avoiding a confrontation. Some objects, like a vehicle (car, bus, truck, or RV), are made of metal and provide excellent shielding if you crouch behind them.

Hiding behind a rock formation also provides decent shielding against an incoming attack.

Objects, like haystacks, provide a place to hide behind, but no protection whatsoever if someone starts shooting at you. With one bullet hit, the haystack will be destroyed, and you'll be vulnerable.

Hiding (crouching down) within a random Bush can keep you from being seen. However, when an enemy determines where you're hiding, a Bush offers zero protection.

Using the Bush loot item allows you to surround yourself with the Bush and move around. You'll truly blend in with your surroundings when you're outside and standing still. As soon as you get noticed, one bullet hit, and the Bush will disappear.

Shown above is what the Bush loot item looks like once it's been activated. Your soldier literally wears the shrub as camouflage.

While wearing a Bush, you can aim and shoot a weapon, but as soon as your soldier gets noticed and shot at, the Bush will no longer keep him/her from being seen. It's always a good idea to shoot at any Bush you come across, especially when you're near the border or have infiltrated the enemy's side of the island. If someone is hiding inside, you'll hit 'em.

If you can't find an object to hide behind, consider building a bunch of pyramid-shaped tiles around you for protection. These are made of wood, so they offer a little bit of protection against bullet attacks, but practically no protection against explosives. Explosive weapons can damage or destroy almost every type of structure, regardless of what it's made from.

Building Is an Essential Skill in *Fortnite: Battle Royale*

Becoming an expert builder, especially in the heat of battle, requires practice, as well as some creativity when it comes to designing structures. Either by watching live streams of expert players on YouTube or Twitch.tv, or by staying in Spectator mode once you're eliminated from a match, watch the final stages of matches carefully to learn the best techniques for building fortresses.

When experiencing a 50 v 50 match, you have plenty of time and safe space to practice building. As many soldiers swarm to a specific location for a firefight, you can always allow your teammates to do the building, and take advantage of what they've built. Each of the small white triangle icons you see here on the main game screen represents one of your teammates.

When you're learning to build in *Fortnite: Battle Royale*, experiment with different structure designs, and develop the skillset needed to be able to build very quickly, without having to think too much about it. If the Playground game play mode is currently offered (it's added and removed from the game periodically), this is the perfect place to practice building.

Each Building Tile Has Its Own Strength

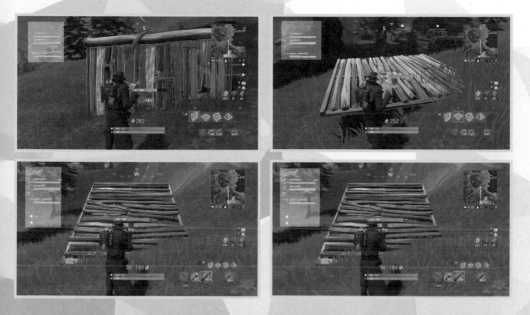

There are four shapes of building tiles—vertical wall tiles, horizontal floor/ceiling tiles, ramp/stair tiles, and pyramid-shaped tiles. Once you enter into Building mode, first choose your building material. Next, decide where you want to build. Finally, one at a time, select which building tile you want to use.

Each tile has an HP level, which determines how much damage it can withstand before collapsing or being destroyed. During the building process, a tile's HP increases gradually. Wood is the fastest to build with, while working with stone is slightly slower. Metal takes the longest to build with but ultimately offers the most protection.

Each tile costs 10 of the selected resource to build. Remember, when you're in Building mode, you can't use a weapon. You'll definitely need to practice quickly switching between Combat mode and Building mode.

Here's a list of the HP strength offered by each tile type once it's fully built. Keep in mind, this information changes slightly when Epic Games tweaks this aspect of the game.

TILE SHAPE	WOOD	STONE	METAL
Horizontal Floor/Ceiling Tile	140 HP	280 HP	460 HP
Vertical Wall Tile	150 HP	300 HP	500 HP
Ramp/Stairs Tile	140 HP	280HP	460 HP
Pyramid-Shaped Tile	140 HP	280HP	460 HP

When you go into Edit mode to alter a tile—to add a door or window, for example—the defensive strength of that tile changes. Each tile has its own HP meter which is displayed when you face the tile.

How to Become a Better Builder

The trick to becoming a highly skilled builder is speed. Achieving speed takes practice! This section contains some additional strategies to help you become an expert builder. In order to build in *Fortnite: Battle Royale*, you must first collect or harvest resources (wood, stone, and metal).

When playing a 50 v 50 game, harvesting resources by smashing objects with your pickaxe generates resources a lot faster.

The resource icons you discover lying on the ground, within chests, within Loot Llamas, and within Supply Drops, allow you to quickly grab larger bundles of specific resources than you'd typically discover in other game play modes. Of course, you can also pick up resources discarded by a defeated enemy when they're eliminated from the match.

First Harvest or Collect Resources and then Build

Large and thick trees can be seen from a distance. When smashing a tree with your pickaxe to harvest wood, if you fully destroy the tree, it crashes to the ground and disappears. This is something that nearby enemies will notice, and it will give away your location. To avoid this, as you're smashing a tree, keep an eye on its HP meter. As soon as it starts to get low, stop smashing the tree (while it's still standing) and move on. You'll still collect wood, but the tree will remain standing. To harvest more wood, simply walk to another tree and repeat the process.

Smashing anything made out of wood that you encounter on the island allows you to harvest wood. Trees and wooden pallets tend to generate a lot of wood. Smashing the walls, floor, or roof of most structures also generates wood, unless the structure is made from a different material.

Smashing anything made of brick or stone generates stone.

Smashing anything made of metal, such as appliances within a home, machinery within a factory or building, or any type of vehicle will generate metal.

Discover Some Useful Building Tips and Strategies

When building a fortress, cover all sides. Don't forget to build a roof to protect you from assaults from above. Wood was used here, but it's the weakest material to build with in terms of defensive strength.

Aside from using a Rocket Launcher, Guided Missile Launcher, or Grenade Launcher from a distance to destroy part of or an entire enemy structure, most types of mid- to long-range shotguns and rifles will work. However, if you can sneak up on the enemy from the ground, attach Remote Explosives to the base of their fort or toss a few Grenades into it, this typically is quicker than continuously shooting at a fortress wall to weaken or destroy it. The screenshot above (on the left) shows a basic metal fortress. The soldier tossed three Grenades through the open door.

As you can see above (on the right), the fortress was quickly destroyed. If an enemy had been hiding out in this structure, he would have been toast. After the explosion, there's no trace left of what was once the metal fortress. Almost any structure on the island can be destroyed with explosives, shot with weapons and damaged (and eventually destroyed), or smashed with a pickaxe. The only way to harvest and collect the resources from it is to use a pickaxe on the structure.

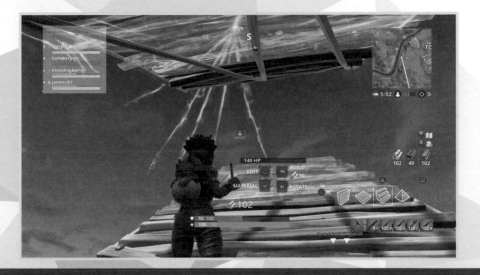

Building an Over-Under Ramp uses twice the resources but allows you to travel up higher (or go down from someplace high up), while protecting yourself from attacks originating above you. As you're building a ramp, position the building cursor in the middle of the upper and lower tiles to build both at the same time.

When you need quick protection, build a vertical wall with the strongest material you have available, and then quickly build a ramp (or stairs) directly behind it. Crouch down behind this structure for protection. Doing this provides a double layer of shielding that an enemy will have to shoot through or destroy in order to reach you. Plus, by crouching down, you become a smaller target.

This is a similar structure (one vertical wall with a ramp behind it), but with vertical walls built on both sides to provide extra protection from flank attacks (from the sides).

In some cases, building two ramps side by side gives you an advantage. An opponent who's below you can't see your exact location when you move back and forth between ramps. Also, if one ramp is about to get destroyed, quickly leap to the other to survive the attack. Yes, this requires more resources, but it's often worth it.

Just one well-aimed Grenade is enough to take down a tall ramp that's made from wood.

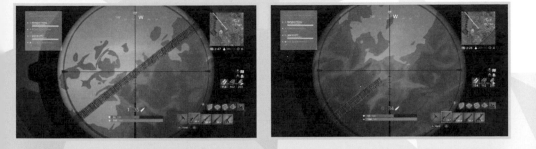

One of the problems with building a very tall ramp is that it's weak. All an enemy needs to do is shoot at the lower or mid-section of the ramp and it'll come crashing down. If a soldier is running up or down the ramp, or standing on it, they too will fall toward the ground and often get injured, especially if the soldier falls from a height of four levels or higher. Destroying a ramp can be done from a distance using a sniper rifle with a scope, a Grenade Launcher, Guided Missile Launcher, or a Rocket Launcher, for example. Any type of fast-shooting weapon (with a high fire rate), such as a machine gun, will also do the trick.

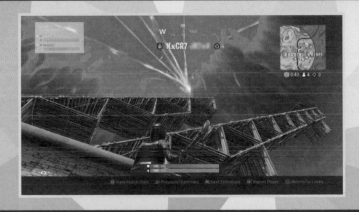

When you have the time and the extra resources, build a well-fortified ramp structure like these. They take longer for enemies to shoot and destroy, so you have longer to reach safety if the ramp gets attacked.

If you see a weakness in a tall structure, and you know an enemy is at or near the top of it, shoot at that weak point. Making the structure collapse will cause your enemy to fall. A short fall will have little impact, but a fall from four (or more) levels up could be devastating. Using explosive weapons will cause the most damage to a structure.

Repeatedly shooting at a structure with a gun's bullets will cause damage and eventually destroy a structure, but this takes longer and requires a lot of ammunition.

As you're shooting at a structure to weaken it, if there's an enemy hiding inside, he or she can use their resources to repair or reinforce the structure. When they do this, you'll need to use even more ammo to ultimately destroy the structure you're shooting at. Unless you have a lot of ammo to waste, you're better off using an explosive weapon to damage or destroy structures.

Learn to Quickly Build "1x1" Fortresses

A 1x1 fortress is simply four walls around you, with a ramp in the center. It goes up multiple levels. Using wood allows you to build with the greatest speed, but using metal offers the greatest protection. Keep practicing until you're able to build this type of fortress very quickly.

An alternative to a 1x1 fortress is to collect and use a Port-A-Fort loot item. These are made of metal and are built instantly when activated. They require no resources. Port-A-Forts are much more common in 50 v 50 matches than in other game play modes.

Here's how to build a 1x1 fortress:

First build one floor tile if the ground is uneven.

Next, build four vertical walls so they surround you.

In the center of the structure, build a ramp. As the ramp is being constructed, jump on it. You've now built one level of a 1x1 fortress.

Repeat these steps until the fortress has reached the desired height.

At the top, consider adding pyramid-shaped roof pieces around the top for added protection when you peek out. However, if you need protection from above as well, add a flat roof and then a pyramid-shaped roof piece directly over your head. This 1x1 fortress is made of metal. It's three levels tall.

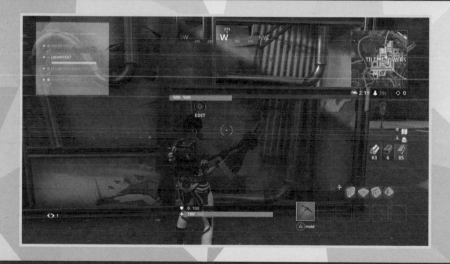

Learning to edit quickly, to add windows, doors, and other customizations to a structure you've built, is an important skill to master. It takes practice to be able to edit structures at lightning-fast speed. To begin editing, face a tile and press the Edit button on your controller or keyboard.

When you're editing a wall tile, choose which of the nine squares you want to remove.

Selecting and then removing one square creates a window. After selecting the tile, press the Confirm key to create the window, or select additional tiles to remove several of them at once, and then use the Confirm command.

Selecting two squares (one on top of the other) creates a door. Removing two squares next to each other creates an extra-wide window.

Any soldier can open and close a door that's been added to a structure. To keep enemies from following you inside your fort, consider adding a Trap inside the fortress on the bottom floor (inside the door).

Edit a floor or ceiling tile to create a hole which you can easily travel through to climb up or down a level within the structure you're building. Start by entering into Edit mode while facing a ground or ceiling tile.

Select one of the squares to remove.

Press the Confirm button to create the hole (in this case, on the floor tile).

When in Edit mode, and while a tile is being constructed, it's semitransparent. Use this to your advantage to see out.

SECTION 3

ESTABLISHING A PERSONAL ARSENAL NEEDED FOR SURVIVAL

There are several ways to gather weapons, ammo, loot items, and resources during your stay on the island. One of your first priorities once you land on the island is to find weapons and build up your arsenal (while staying on your team's side of the island).

Once you've built up your arsenal and you're ready for battle, travel toward the border to seek out enemies when playing a 50 v 50 match. You can always tell where the intense battles are taking place by checking the island map and looking for a cluster of blue triangles (which represent your teammates) near the border. If you want enemies to seek you out to initiate a firefight, simply cross the border and enter into enemy territory.

Keep Your Eyes Peeled for Chests, Supply Drops, Loot Llamas, and Vending Machines

Some weapons and ammo can be found lying out in the open (on the ground).

Throughout the island—mainly within buildings, homes, and other structures, as well as inside of trucks, but sometimes out in the open—you'll discover chests.

Chests have a golden glow and make a sound when you get close to them. Open chests to collect a random selection of weapons, ammo, loot items, and resources. To collect a chest's contents, you must be the first soldier to open it during a match.

Some chests are usually found at the same spot on the map match after match, although this is changing as Epic Games releases new game updates. Sometimes, chests randomly appear during each match, so always be on the lookout for them (and listen carefully for the sound they make).

As you're exploring various areas, listen closely for the unique sound chests emit. You'll often hear this sound before a chest comes into view. Assuming it's safe, approach the chest and open it. Then be ready to grab the items you want or need. Anytime you're searching a home, you'll often find one or more chests in an attic, basement, or garage. Sometimes, they're just sitting out in the open.

If you're within the circle that's displayed on the island map, at random times during a match, you may be lucky enough to spot Supply Drops. These are floating balloons with a wooden crate attached to them. When you spot one, approach with caution, and open the crate. Inside you'll discover a random selection of weapons, loot items, ammo, and resource icons.

An even rarer object to come across on the island is a Loot Llama. This colorful item looks like a piñata. Open it and you'll discover a collection of random weapons, ammo, loot items, and resource icons. Typically, the weapons found within Loot Llamas are rare and often "legendary."

Instead of opening a Loot Llama, if it's close to the border where enemies will be lurking, an alternate strategy is to place Remote Explosives on it and then hide. As soon as an enemy soldier approaches, manually detonate the explosives to defeat the enemy. As you approach a Supply Drop or Loot Llama, consider quickly building walls around yourself and the object so you're protected before opening the crate or smashing the Loot Llama.

Scattered randomly throughout the island are Vending Machines. Exchange resources you've collected to acquire any of the weapons or loot items being offered. Each Vending Machine offers a different selection of items that can be purchased using wood, stone, or metal. If there's something being offered by a Vending Machine that you don't have enough resources to purchase, go off and collect the needed resources. Here, the soldier wanted to purchase a Rocket Launcher for 400 metal. He only had 30 metal in his personal arsenal.

By smashing a bunch of nearby vehicles and other metal items, accumulating plenty of metal here in Tilted Towers was not much of a challenge, and it took less than 3 minutes.

After collecting the needed 400 metal, this soldier was the proud owner of an "Epic" Rocket Launcher. It also came with a supply of ammunition. Because this soldier's backpack was already full, the next step was to drop one of the weapons he no longer wanted to free up space for the Rocket Launcher. With less than 2 minutes before the storm would arrive at his location, this soldier now needed to book it and head toward the circle.

In addition to being able to view your soldier's inventory and arsenal on the main game screen, the Backpack Inventory screen allows you to see additional information and learn more about a particular weapon or ammo type. From this screen, you're also able to reorganize which backpack slot a particular weapon or item is in. This is useful because it allows you to make your favorite, or most frequently used, weapons more easily accessible.

What your soldier is currently carrying is normally shown on the right side of the screen. The location where this information is displayed will vary based on which gaming system you're using. You can always view this information. Switching to the Backpack Inventory is not always feasible, especially during an intense firefight, because you're prevented from seeing and controlling your soldier.

At any time, your soldier's backpack can hold six items (including the pickaxe). That leaves five slots in which you can carry different types of guns, alternative weapons (such as Remote Explosives or Grenades), and/or powerup loot items (such as Med Kits, Chug Jugs, Shield Potions, Bandages, or Slurp Juice).

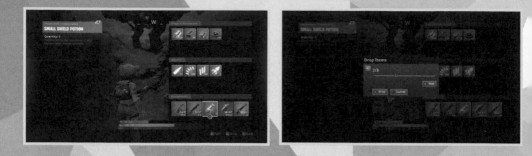

Another thing you can do from the Backpack Inventory screen is drop a weapon, loot item, or resources. Do this to free up an inventory slot in your backpack, or to share an item (or resources) with a teammate. Select the weapon, ammo type, loot item, or resource you want to drop, and then press the Drop button. Here, the Small Shield Potion is selected.

If you're holding a quantity of a specific type of ammo, loot item, or resource, when you choose to drop it, this pop-up window appears. It allows you to choose how much of what you have on hand you want to share (drop). Here, using the slider, two of the three Small Shield Potions the soldier was holding were dropped and given to a teammate.

Finding weapons and loot items, and then building your arsenal is just one part of the overall challenge. You'll also need to choose the perfect weapon to use, based on the situation you're currently facing, and then ensure you have ample ammunition for that weapon.

There are several different types of ammunition to collect. Each works with a different category of weapon. Remember, without ammunition, a weapon is useless. When you run out of ammo, a message stating, "Not Enough Ammo" and/or "Out of Ammo!" appears on the screen, plus your soldier will shake his or her head when you try to shoot.

What You Should Know About Weapons

The weapon categories that firearms and explosives typically fall into include: Rifles, Grenade Launchers, Grenades, Miniguns, Pistols, Rocket Launchers, Shotguns, SMGs (Sub Machine Guns), and Sniper Rifles. Other types of weapons are always being introduced into the game.

Many *Fortnite: Battle Royale* gamers agree that the most versatile weapon to master is any type of shotgun. There are several types of shotguns to be found within the game. They can be used in close-range or mid-range combat situations, or even at a distance. (From a distance, they're harder to aim accurately than a rifle with a scope, for example.) When using a shotgun, always try for a headshot to inflict the most damage. Each category of weapon can be used for a different purpose.

When experiencing a 50 v 50 match, you'll likely need to rely on more powerful weapons, especially if you join a bunch of your teammates in an intense battle against a group of enemies. The distance you are from your target needs to be considered when choosing the right weapon to use. Most close- and mid-range weapons, for example, lose accuracy and cause less damage the farther away you are from your target.

Three Tips to Improve Your Shooting Accuracy

Regardless of which weapon you're using, your aim improves when you crouch down and press the Aim button for the weapon you're using.

When using most weapons, anytime you press the Aim button before the trigger button, you'll zoom in a bit on your opponent and have more precise control over the positioning of the weapon's targeting crosshairs. Your shooting accuracy will improve.

While it's often necessary to be running or jumping at the same time you're firing a weapon, your accuracy definitely improves when you're standing still.

You almost always have an advantage when you're higher up than your opponent and shooting in a downward direction.

A rifle with a scope (or a thermal scope) will come in handy anytime during a match for spying on your enemies from a distance. Even if you're short on ammo for this weapon and need to conserve it, use this weapon as a fancy set of binoculars to spy on distant targets. When viewing a target through a scope, you can really zoom in from a distance.

A thermal scope allows you to see through walls and spot hiding enemies. The yellow figures near the center of the crosshairs are enemy soldiers running in the distance. Using a scoped rifle allows you to shoot at your targets from a distance with extreme accuracy. One drawback to this weapon is that it typically holds just a few shells (bullets) at a time before it needs to be reloaded.

A trick when using a rifle with a slow reload time and small capacity is to carry two of them in your backpack, place them in slots next to each other, and then quickly switch between the two weapons when one needs to reload. Make sure you have a safe place to crouch down and hide during the weapon's reload period.

Understand How Weapons Are Rated and Categorized

While every weapon has the ability to cause damage and potentially defeat your adversaries, each is rated based on several criteria, including its rarity. Weapons are color-coded with a hue around them to showcase their rarity. Remember, each type of weapon will require practice as you learn to accurately aim and use it.

Weapons with a **grey** hue are "Common."

Weapons with a **green** hue are "Uncommon."

Weapons with a **blue** hue are "Rare."

Weapons with a **purple** hue are "Epic."

Weapons with an **orange** hue are "Legendary." They tend to be harder to find, extra powerful, and very rare. If you're able to obtain one, grab it! When experiencing a 50 v 50 match, you're most apt to find "legendary" weapons within Supply Drops or by defeating enemies. They do periodically show up elsewhere, however.

It is possible to collect several of the same weapon, but each could have a different rarity. So, if you collect two of the same weapon type, and one is rare, but the second is legendary, definitely keep the legendary weapon and trade the other for something else when you find a replacement.

Learn About the Power of Weapons and the Damage Each Can Cause

If you're really interested in how a weapon is rated, evaluate its DPS (Damage Per Second) rating, overall Damage Rating, Fire Rate, MAG (Magazine) Capacity, and Reload Time. This is information that Epic Games tweaks often. Select a weapon when viewing your Backpack Inventory screen to see details about it.

There are plenty of websites, including: IGN.com (www.ign.com/wikis/fortnite/Weapons), Gameskinny.com (www.gameskinny.com/9mt22/complete-fortnite-battle-royale-weapons-stats-list), and RankedBoost.com (https://rankedboost.com/fortnite/best-weapons-tier-list), that provide the current stats for each weapon offered in *Fortnite: Battle Royale*, based on the latest tweaks made to the game. Just make sure when you look at this information online, it refers to the most recently released version of *Fortnite: Battle Royale*.

Choose Your Arsenal Wisely

Based on where you are, what challenges you're currently facing, the distance you are from your target(s), and what you anticipate your needs will be, stock your backpack with the weapons and tools you believe you'll need.

The various types of ammunition you've collected, how much of each ammo type you have on hand, and which weapons each ammo type can be used with, is also displayed on the Backpack Inventory screen. While viewing this screen, select a specific ammunition type to learn more about it. Here you can see that Heavy Bullets has been selected from the Backpack Inventory screen, and that this soldier has six of these high caliber bullets on hand.

Some weapons, like pistols, are ideal for close-range firefights, but are relatively weak. Other weapons (like shotguns) are better suited for close- to mid-range combat. Rifles with a scope allow you to shoot at enemies from a distance. Projectile explosive weapons (like Rocket Launchers) are ideal for destroying structures and/or enemies that are far away. It's important to find and carry an assortment of weapons so you're able to deal with any fighting situation you encounter.

How and Where to Collect Ammo

The different types of ammunition include:

- **Heavy Bullets**—Used in sniper rifles and other high-caliber weapons that are designed for long-range shooting.
- **Light Bullets**—Used in pistols, SMGs, and most handheld guns. This type of ammo causes more damage when used at close range. To inflict the most damage, aim for a headshot or hit your target multiple times.
- **Medium Bullets**—Used in assault rifles and similar weapons. This type of ammo is ideal for mid-range shooting, although the closer you are, the more damage each bullet will inflict.
- **Rockets**—This is long-range explosive ammunition that's used with Rocket Launchers, Guided Missile Launchers, and Grenade Launchers. Even if you don't yet have one of these weapons in your personal arsenal, collect this ammo whenever you can and stockpile it. You can always share it with your teammates. Having a Rocket Launcher, Guided Missile Launcher, or Grenade Launcher will be extremely useful during the End Game.
- **Shells**—Used in shotguns. This ammo will inflict the most damage at close range, but shotguns can be used when you're at any distance from your target. The farther you are away, the less damage each direct hit will inflict.

Without having the appropriate ammunition on hand, whatever weapons you're carrying will be useless. Throughout each match, there are several ways to find and collect ammo.

Ammunition can be collected from Ammo Boxes. These are scattered throughout the island, and often found within structures on shelves or hidden behind objects. Unlike chests, they do not glow or make a sound.

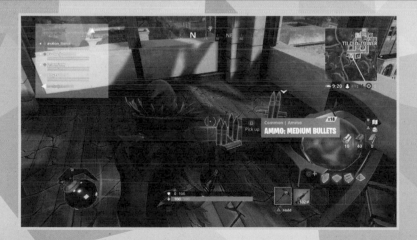

Random types of ammunition can sometimes be found out in the open, lying on the ground. Sometimes the ammo is alone, but often, it's found in conjunction with a compatible weapon.

You can often grab a nice assortment of ammunition that a soldier drops, immediately after they've been defeated and eliminated from a match.

Chests, Supply Drops, and Loot Llamas often contain random collections of ammunition. From the chest shown here, 72 Medium Bullets are about to be collected, along with a few other useful items, including Bandages.

Finding, Collecting, and Using Loot Items

There are many types of loot items available to you during a match. Some are very rare, while others you'll be able to collect often. Each type of loot item serves one of four purposes.

- **Weapons**—Traps, Grenades, Stink Bombs, Impulse Grenades, and Remote Explosives are examples of items that get collected and are used against enemies when needed. Some of these items require an inventory slot within your backpack. Others, like Traps, get stored along with your resources. In most cases, you can carry multiples of the same item, such as three or six Grenades, within the same backpack inventory slot.

- **Tools**—Items like a Port-A-Fort or Bush can be useful to aid in your survival.

- **Health and/or Shield Powerups**—Med Kits, Chug Jugs, Bandages, Shield Potions, and Slurp Juice, for example, can be used to replenish your Health meter and/or activate and then replenish your Shield meter. Each of these items takes time to consume or use, during which time your soldier will be vulnerable to attack.

- **Transportation**—Shopping Carts, Bouncers, Launch Pads, Rift-to-Go items, and All Terrain Karts are examples of items that can randomly be found throughout the island and that will help you travel around.

Displayed near the bottom-center of the screen on most gaming systems are your Health and Shield meters. Both meters max out at 100. Your soldier's Health meter (displayed as a green bar) starts at 100 and decreases each time your soldier gets injured from the storm, an enemy attack, or a fall, for example. Your soldier's Shield meter (displayed as a blue bar) starts at zero. You must find and use some type of loot item powerup to activate your shields and boost them up to a maximum of 100. Shields do not protect your soldier from the storm or falls. They do offer additional protection from bullets and explosions.

Traps can be used to booby trap any type of structure, such as a room in a house, a fortress you've built, or a ramp. Once you grab a Trap, it gets stored with your resources, not your weapons, so Traps do not take up a slot in your backpack.

To access a Trap that you're carrying, switch into Building mode, press the appropriate button on your controller/keyboard to select it, and then place the Trap on a wall, floor, or ceiling, for example, where you want to set it. To set the Trap, press the Place Trap button on your controller/keyboard. If you're carrying several different kinds of Traps, scroll through them and choose which one to use in a particular situation.

Most loot items can be found within chests, Supply Drops, and Loot Llamas, as well as lying out in the open (often on the ground). Loot items can also be acquired after you defeat an enemy—when he or she drops everything they were carrying after being eliminated from the match. Some items can also be obtained from Vending Machines (by exchanging resources you've collected within the game).

SECTION 4

WORKING WITH YOUR TEAM TO ACHIEVE #1 VICTORY ROYALE

When choosing a landing spot during a 50 v 50 match, pick a place that's not right on the border. You're better off being a slight distance away, building up your arsenal once you land, and then moving toward the circle, where the action is.

Survival Strategies That Are Ideal for 50 v 50 Matches

The following is a collection of strategies that'll help you stay alive longer during 50 v 50 matches so you can contribute to your team and help it achieve #1 Victory Royale.

If you are hanging around and exploring close to the border (even if you're nowhere near the circle), there's a good chance enemy soldiers will spot you, cross the border, and attack.

Anytime you look at the Location Map or Island Map, if you spot a bunch of your teammates running toward the same location, this is often where a battle is currently taking place. If you want to fight, follow them to that location. Otherwise, stay clear of that area.

Shortly after you land, the island map will display the location of the circle. It's within this region that Supply Drops will fall. Some will be on your team's side of the border, some will land on the opposite side. Regardless of the landing location, be careful as you approach Supply Drops. Enemy snipers could take you out from a distance, or enemy soldiers could be hiding nearby waiting to launch a surprise attack.

It's around the circle that the Final Circle will ultimately take place as the match draws to an end. If you remain alive long enough, you'll need to outrun the storm and eventually reach this area to participate in the End Game.

Once you're in or near the Final Circle area, you'll discover your team-mates and rivals have already done a lot of building. Take advantage of these structures, without having to waste time and resources building yourself.

When healing one of your teammates, watch out for an enemy who might sneak up behind you and then eliminate you both from the match. It's particularly hard to hear footsteps if you're in the middle of a battle and gunshots and explosions are happening all around you. Surround yourself with walls to provide protection, if necessary.

During a 50 v 50 match, avoid wearing a large, bright-colored outfit, like the Cuddle Team Leader outfit. Bright-colored outfits are much easier for your enemy to spot during a battle. You'll put unnecessary attention on yourself, plus make your soldier a bigger target during the End Game. As this soldier approaches the Final Circle and is out in the open, she's being shot at.

Anytime you're playing a 50 v 50 match, unless you have a reason to talk to your squad mates or partner during the match, turn off the microphone on your gaming headset. When you are using the microphone to speak with fellow gamers, turn off any music playing in the background and avoid unnecessary conversation with people you're around in the real world so you don't disturb your fellow gamers. If you want to listen to music or chat with other people who are not playing *Fortnite: Battle Royale*, mute your microphone!

You don't need to be right in the heart of the action to make a vital contribution to a battle. This soldier is far away from the turmoil, but he spotted an enemy soldier building up a fortress in the distance.

By quickly shooting the ramp area of the structure multiple times in quick succession, the fortress was destroyed. During the End Game shown here, only two enemy soldiers remained, and the soldier you're looking at helped defeat one of them.

As you can see from this island map, the Final Circle is quickly shrinking during this End Game. Notice the cluster of your teammates in the heart of the circle, right at the border. Here 26 of your teammates remain in play, while 15 enemies are still alive. The circle closes in again in 45 seconds. Armed with a rifle that has a scope, the soldier being controlled in this match is away from his teammates, but using the scope, he is sniping at enemies from a distance, so he's actually well positioned and making a valuable contribution to the team.

As the End Game approaches, being right at the border and standing out in the open in the middle of Loot Lake is not a smart move. Yes, there are some powerful weapons that can be grabbed here (because another soldier perished), but moving around in water is a slow process, and there's no place for this soldier to take cover if an enemy starts shooting. A smarter approach would have been to build a wooden bridge over the water to reach these weapons.

Here's another example of a soldier who is armed with a sniper rifle with a scope (and 109 remaining bullets for it). He positions himself a good distance away from where the battle is really heating up. You can see the massive cluster of teammates near the border by looking at the Location Map in the corner of the screen.

This soldier, however, has a perfect line-of-sight view of an enemy fortress, and is able to shoot at enemies as they peek their heads out of the fortress. By shooting repeatedly at the fort, walls can be torn down, but the enemies within that fort can quickly rebuild and repair them.

As you're approaching the main battle zone, when you need to travel across vast and open spaces run (don't walk) in a zigzag pattern and keep jumping in order to make yourself a difficult and moving target to hit.

In addition to collecting weapons, as soon as you land, be on the lookout for Shield Potions (or a shield-related powerup) and use one or two of them. This will activate your shields.

If you're in the mood to take some risk, after landing, head directly into the circle and hope you're able to either gather awesome weapons from a Supply Drop or pick up what soldiers drop after they've been eliminated from the match in order to build your personal arsenal. You'll definitely encounter some enemies doing this. As you approach the circle, look up and you'll likely see several Supply Drops in the sky.

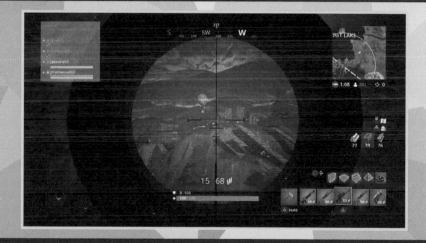

Once you obtain a sniper rifle (with a scope) try to reach the circle (and the border) as early as possible. Find a high-up place where you can see around you. Wait for Supply Drops to fall, and then target all of the enemies that approach the Supply Drops. Remember, you can do this from a distance, yet still have precise aim when using a sniper rifle. A Rocket Launcher, Guided Missile Launcher, or Grenade Launcher will also work.

If you come across a Chug Jug, hold on to it until the End Game. You'll likely take damage during an intense fight and will want the health and shield boost, especially after you get revived by a teammate. When consumed, a Chug Jug boosts your health and shields back to 100. It takes 15 seconds to consume one of these powerups, so make sure you're in a safe place before using it.

Pay attention to the storm! Once you land, it's easy to get caught up in exploration and building your arsenal to the point where you lose track of time and where you are. The storm's movement starts after 10 minutes and then it keeps moving and expanding rather quickly. If you don't want to worry about the storm's progress, make your way to the circle early. When you notice the storm appearing within your Location Map, it's close and likely moving in quickly. You'd better follow the white line to avoid the damage the storm will cause if you get caught in it.

During your freefall from the Battle Bus, if you notice the circle forms far away from your intended landing location, make a sharp turn and head closer to the circle. Otherwise, you'll have a long trek toward the circle once the storm begins to expand.

Assuming you're not the first one from your team headed to the circle, if there's a steep cliff that needs to be climbed along the way, chances are one of your teammates has already built a ramp. If you spot the ramp from a distance, take a detour to use it so you don't need to waste resources building your own.

When you need to get down from the top of a tall hill or steep cliff, don't jump off! You'll get injured or could perish. Instead, slide down and you'll arrive at the bottom safely.

If you notice your health and/or shields are getting low, you're close to the border, and you know that you'll be encountering enemies any moment, take a quick break to drink a Chug Jug, or use another health and/or shields powerup to boost your levels.

Here, the End Game is well under way. One team still has 32 survivors ready to do battle. The opposing team has just two. There's a maze of buildings and structures all around within the Final Circle, so it'll take a sharp eye to find and defeat those last two enemies.

Stepping into a Rift allows your soldier to go airborne and then use a glider to coast through the air and safely land. Use this as a quick way to travel a far distance. For example, if you're in the heart of the Paradise Palms desert area and need to get closer to the circle quickly. Using a Rift-to-Go item allows you to create and use a Rift on demand wherever you happen to be.

Other modes of transportation that are faster than running include riding in a Shopping Cart, using a Bounce Pad, stepping onto a Launch Pad, or driving an All Terrain Kart (ATK). These souped-up golf carts are most often found within the Paradise Palms or Lazy Links areas of the island. Keep in mind, up to four teammates can ride in an ATK at once. While the driver cannot shoot weapons while driving, all three passengers can use their weapons. The back of an ATK can also serve as a Bouncer Pad. Keep in mind, enemies can shoot at ATKs, potentially destroy them, and at the same time, injure or defeat its occupants.

One of the great things about participating in a 50 v 50 match is that you don't need to be the one defeating all of the enemies in order to enjoy a #1 Victory Royale. You just need to stay alive and help out your team as much as possible.

SECTION 5
FORTNITE: BATTLE ROYALE RESOURCES

On YouTube (www.youtube.com) or Twitch.tv (www.twitch.tv/direc-tory/game/Fortnite), in the Search field, enter the search phrase *"Fortnite: Battle Royale"* or *"Fortnite 50 v 50 Matches"* to discover many game-related channels, live streams, and prerecorded videos that'll help you become a better player.

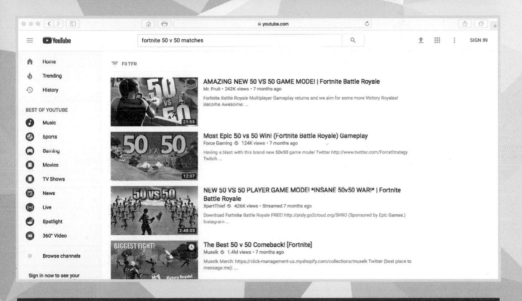

This is just a sampling of the entertaining and informative videos you'll find on YouTube when you enter the search phrase *"Fortnite 50 v 50 Match."*

Also, be sure to check out these other online resources:

WEBSITE OR YOUTUBE CHANNEL NAME	DESCRIPTION	URL
Fandom's Fortnite Wiki	Discover the latest news and strategies related to *Fortnite: Battle Royale*.	http://fortnite.wikia.com/wiki/Fortnite_Wiki
FantasticalGamer	A popular YouTuber who publishes *Fortnite* tutorial videos.	www.youtube.com/user/FantasticalGamer
FBR Insider	The *Fortnite: Battle Royale Insider* website offers game-related news, tips, and strategy videos.	www.fortniteinsider.com
Fortnite Gamepedia Wiki	Read up-to-date descriptions of every weapon, loot item, and ammo type available within *Fortnite: Battle Royale*. This Wiki also maintains a comprehensive database of soldier outfits and related items released by Epic Games.	https://fortnite.gamepedia.com/Fortnite_Wiki
Fortnite Intel	An independent source of news related to *Fortnite: Battle Royale*.	www.fortniteintel.com
Fortnite Scout	Check your personal player stats, and analyze your performance using a bunch of colorful graphs and charts. Also check out the stats of other *Fortnite: Battle Royale* players.	www.fortnitescout.com
Fortnite Stats & Leaderboard	This is an independent website that allows you to view your own *Fortnite*-related stats or discover the stats from the best players in the world.	https://fortnitestats.com
Game Informer Magazine's *Fortnite* Coverage	Discover articles, reviews, and news about *Fortnite: Battle Royale* published by *Game Informer* magazine.	www.gameinformer.com/search/searchresults.aspx?q=Fortnite

Game Skinny Online Guides	A collection of topic-specific strategy guides related to *Fortnite*.	www.gameskinny.com/tag/fortnite-guides/
GameSpot's *Fortnite* Coverage	Check out the news, reviews, and game coverage related to *Fortnite: Battle Royale* that's been published by GameSpot.	www.gamespot.com/fortnite
IGN Entertainment's *Fortnite* Coverage	Check out all IGN's past and current coverage of *Fortnite*.	www.ign.com/wikis/fortnite
Jason R. Rich's Website and Social Media Feeds	Share your *Fortnite: Battle Royale* game play strategies with this book's author and learn about his other books.	www.JasonRich.com www.FortniteGameBooks.com Twitter: @JasonRich7 Instagram: @JasonRich7
Microsoft's Xbox One *Fortnite* Website	Learn about and acquire *Fortnite: Battle Royale* if you're an Xbox One gamer.	www.microsoft.com/en-US/store/p/Fortnite-Battle-Royalee/BT5P2X999VH2
MonsterDface YouTube and Twitch.tv Channels	Watch video tutorials and live game streams from an expert *Fortnite* player.	www.youtube.com/user/MonsterdfaceLive www.Twitch.tv/MonsterDface
Ninja	Check out the live and recorded game streams from Ninja, one of the most highly skilled *Fortnite: Battle Royale* players in the world on Twitch.tv and YouTube.	www.twitch.tv/ninja_fortnite_hyper www.youtube.com/user/NinjasHyper
Nomxs	A YouTube and Twitch.tv channel hosted by online personality Simon Britton (Nomxs). He too is one of *Fortnite*'s top-ranked players.	https://youtu.be/np-8cmsUZmc or www.twitch.tv/videos/259245155
Official Epic Games YouTube Channel for *Fortnite: Battle Royale*	The official *Fortnite: Battle Royale* YouTube channel.	www.youtube.com/user/epicfortnite
Turtle Beach Corp.	This is one of many companies that make great quality, wired or wireless (Bluetooth) gaming headsets that work with all gaming platforms.	www.turtlebeach.com

Your *Fortnite: Battle Royale* Adventure Continues . . .

If you're trying to become a better all-around *Fortnite: Battle Royale* player, it's going to require a lot of practice. You'll need to participate in many matches, and continuously work on perfecting your fighting, exploration, and building skills. You're going to be defeated many times. Don't get frustrated or discouraged by defeats! Over time, you'll begin to survive longer during matches and fine-tune your skills so you're able to defeat more and more enemies on your own.

Participating in 50 v 50 matches is one of the best ways to improve your gaming skills, while getting the chance to explore different areas of the island and test out some of the rarer weapons and loot items that are typically very hard to come by during a Solo, Duos, or Squads match, for example.

To improve your *Fortnite: Battle Royale* gaming skills, spend extra time in the early stages of each match on your team's side of the border— well away from enemies and the threat of attack. This will give you extra time to explore, collect resources, and practice building, or you can use the time to gather a powerful arsenal and work to improve your aim using various types of weapons.

When you're ready to really put your fighting skills to the test, head into the circle and you'll be able to confront a multitude of enemies head on, while hopefully having the support of your teammates nearby. Remember, you're rewarded for sharing your weapons, ammo, loot items, and resources, as well as for reviving your teammates who get injured, so be a team player.

Playing 50 v 50 matches is exciting, fun, and challenging, but it offers a vastly different experience than when you're playing a Solo, Duo, or Squads match. If Epic Games is offering a 50 v 50 Squads game play mode, when you select it, you're able to team up with up to three of your online friends to form a four-person squad.

Your squad becomes part of a 50-soldier team, but the four of you can communicate during the match using gaming headsets, and work on planning and executing perfectly timed and well-coordinated attacks. When you're teamed up with your squad, try to find enemies that are on their own to confront so you can easily outnumber and outgun them.

The most important thing when playing every *Fortnite: Battle Royale* 50 v 50 match is to have fun, and of course, try to help your team achieve #1 Victory Royale!